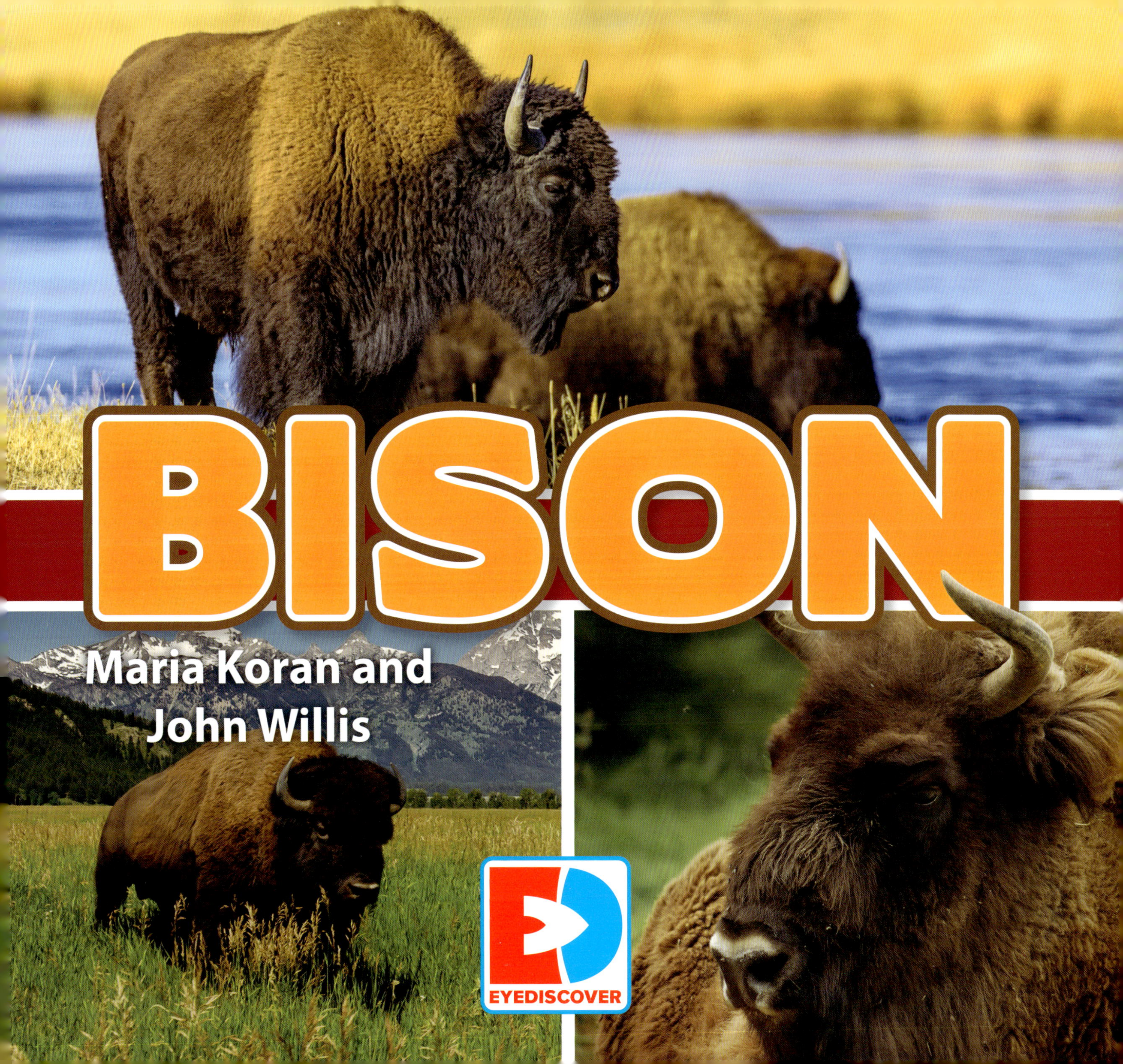
BISON
Maria Koran and
John Willis
EYEDISCOVER

Go to **www.eyediscover.com** and enter this book's unique code.

BOOK CODE

AVS87593

EYEDISCOVER brings you optic readalongs that support active learning.

Published by Lightbox Learning Inc.
276 5th Avenue, Suite 704 #917
New York, NY 10001
Website: www.eyediscover.com

Library of Congress Control Number: 2021937115

ISBN 978-1-7911-3988-9 (hardcover)

Printed in Guangzhou, China
3 4 5 6 7 8 9 0 26 25 24 23 22

082022
220728

Project Coordinator: John Willis
Designer: Mandy Christiansen

The publisher acknowledges Getty Images and Alamy as the primary image suppliers for this title.

EYEDISCOVER provides enriched content, optimized for tablet use, that supplements and complements this book. EYEDISCOVER books strive to create inspired learning and engage young minds in a total learning experience.

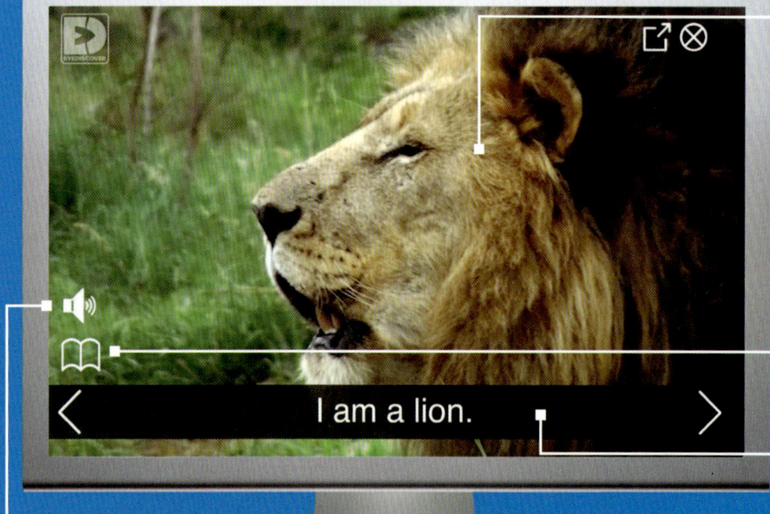

Watch
Video content brings each page to life.

Browse
Thumbnails make navigation simple.

Read
Follow along with text on the screen.

Listen
Hear each page read aloud.

Your EYEDISCOVER Optic Readalongs come alive with...

Audio
Listen to the entire book read aloud.

Video
High resolution videos turn each spread into an optic readalong.

OPTIMIZED FOR
- TABLETS
- WHITEBOARDS
- COMPUTERS
- AND MUCH MORE!

This title is part of our EyeDiscover digital subscription

1-Year EyeDiscover Subscription
ISBN 978-1-4896-8346-5

Access all EyeDiscover titles with our digital subscription.
Sign up for a FREE trial at **www.eyediscover.com/trial**

In this book, you will learn about

- where it is
- what it looks like
- how it lives

and much more!

Bison are the largest land animals in North America.

Bison are sometimes called buffalo. This is because they look like another animal with that name.

Bison look slow, but they can move very fast. A bison may run as fast as a horse.

Bison are found in plains and forests. They live in groups called herds.

All bison grow two horns. Bison use their horns to keep safe and to compete with each other.

Bison grow long coats in winter. This helps them keep warm.

A bison mother has one baby at a time. Baby bison are called calves.

Bison only eat plants.
Most of their food
comes from grass
and herbs.

Bison almost disappeared when people hunted them. Today, most bison live in protected areas.

There are about **30,000** **wild bison** living in protected areas of **North America**.

There once were more than **50 million bison** in North America. By **1889**, there were **only about 1,000**.

A BISON can weigh 2,000 POUNDS (907 kg).

A bison can jump about 6 feet (1.8 m) in the air.

About 400,000 bison live on farms across North America.

A newborn bison calf can weigh up to 70 pounds (32 kg).

KEY WORDS

Research has shown that as much as 65 percent of all written material published in English is made up of 300 words. These 300 words cannot be taught using pictures or learned by sounding them out. They must be recognized by sight. This book contains 57 common sight words to help young readers improve their reading fluency and comprehension. This book also teaches young readers several important content words, such as proper nouns. These words are paired with pictures to aid in learning and improve understanding.

Page	Sight Words First Appearance
4	America, animals, are, in, land, the
7	another, because, is, like, look, name, sometimes, that, they, this, with
8	a, as, but, can, may, move, run, very
11	and, found, groups, live
12	all, each, grow, keep, other, their, to, two, use
15	helps, long, them
16	at, has, mother, one, time
19	comes, eat, food, from, most, of, only, plants
20	almost, people, when

Page	Content Words First Appearance
4	bison, North America
7	buffalo
8	horse
11	forests, herds, plains
12	horns
15	coats, winter
16	baby, calves
19	grass, herbs

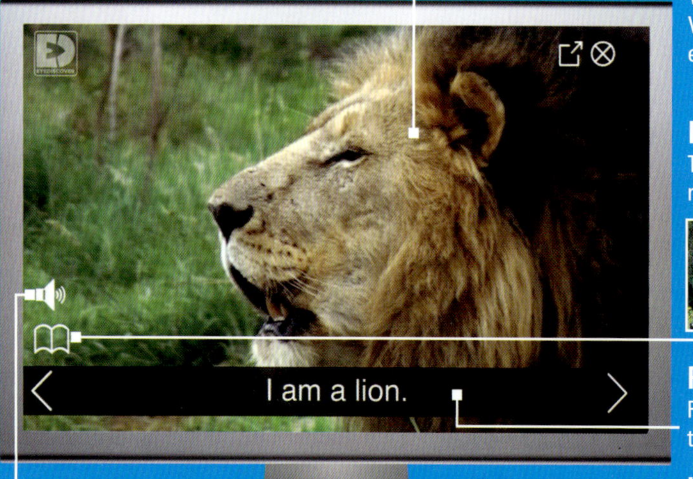

Watch
Video content brings each page to life.

Browse
Thumbnails make navigation simple.

Read
Follow along with text on the screen.

Listen
Hear each page read aloud.

Go to www.eyediscover.com and enter this book's unique code.

BOOK CODE

AVS87593